GEORGE MELVIN FRESE, PE

LOST HISTORY AND A BIZARRE MYSTERY

MAY, 1944-AUGUST, 1946

iUniverse, Inc.
Bloomington

LOST HISTORY AND A BIZARRE MYSTERY
May, 1944-August, 1946

iUniverse books may be ordered through booksellers or by contacting:

iUniverse
1663 Liberty Drive
Bloomington, IN 47403
www.iuniverse.com
1-800-Authors (1-800-288-4677)

ISBN: 978-1-4759-4143-2 (sc)
ISBN: 978-1-4759-4309-2 (hc)
ISBN: 978-1-4759-4144-9 (ebk)

Library of Congress Control Number: 2012914035

Printed in the United States of America

iUniverse rev. date: 08/09/2012

Lost History and a Bizarre Mystery
May 1944 - August 1946

Prologue

The incentive for me in writing this story is to tell about some important events in history that occurred in Berlin, Germany, immediately following the Allies victory which ended World War II in Europe. These events were top secret at the time and were key events that helped shape our history. I believe that some of this history could be lost, if I do not properly record it in this writing.

The mystery to me was, and still is, how I found myself in the right place, at the right time, to observe these events and then be able to offer my skill and service exactly when they were needed. I have tried to review my life and trace the steps of my experience and training that led me to be right where my help was needed. In the Epilog, I will retrace the earliest events in my life that made this story possible.

Table of Contents

Chapter 1
No Assignment

The history in this book occurred immediately after World War II. It was a time of great turmoil between Russia and the United States, France, and England. After the war, the Allied Forces could not agree on what to do with Berlin. The tension between the US President, Harry Truman, and the Russian leader, Joseph Stalin, was so great that all communications between the two governments were top secret. Consequently, none of these happenings were ever in the news. My hope is that this book will help fill in some of these gaps in history.

The mystery will become apparent as the story unfolds. I became aware that I was someone totally out of the ordinary at the time I was drafted into the Army in May 1944. The war was going very badly for the United States and we were losing more men than could be replaced by the draft. All draftees were assigned to the Infantry with no exceptions. Out of the 2,000 men I was drafted with, I was the only one given a different assignment. I was sent to the Signal Corps at Camp Crowder, Missouri, for Basic Training. It was not unnoticed by all the other draftees, for when my assignment was announced, a huge "boo" went up in the crowd and there were shouts of "Congressman's son." I wondered why I wasn't sent to the infantry like everyone else.

Immediately I was given Corporal stripes as a non-commissioned officer. All of the other men in Basic Training with me were Buck Privates. Why I was made a Corporal as soon as I arrived at Basic Training was a mystery to me.

Corporal George Frese at Basic Training

Upon graduation from Basic Training, all of the privates were assigned to units, but I was assigned to Officer Candidate School (OCS) in Fort Monmouth, New Jersey. At OCS, we were given an orange arm band to put on our left sleeve. This band meant we were all to be called "Mister" and all treated the same. Up to this point I was still within the military system of law, and I did just as I was told.

OCS was tough. We would get up at four o'clock in the morning and go for a two hour run. It was winter, so it was cold out at 4 am. Then we would have breakfast, followed by our classes, with a half hour for lunch and a half hour for dinner. We continued classes until 10:30 pm. Lights were out at 12:00 pm. So, we were getting about four hours of sleep each night. Our classroom training went on for three months. Then we had a month of training working and sleeping in the field. At OCS, if you received ten demerits, you were kicked out of the school. Many of my bunkmates got ten demerits. The next day they rolled up their blankets and were out of there. I got my 10th demerit, but no orders to leave. I got my 11th, 12th, 13th, but still no orders to go. Why was I treated differently?

Keeping up with this schedule at OCS was tough, so tough that I wanted out. I did not like getting up at four in the morning, going for a run, and then spending the rest of the day in classes learning about all these topics that you needed to know to be an officer. I decided that since I had already gotten too many demerits, would likely not graduate, why should I continue to work so hard? So I reported to the Major's office, saluted him, pointed my finger at his nose, and said, "Sir, I want out of this chicken shit outfit." I figured that should get me out.

He pointed his finger at me and said loudly and with a stern tone, "You do not tell the Army what you want to do! The Army tells you what you are going to do. And the Army is telling you! You are going back to class, and you are going to work harder than ever. That's an order!" As he spoke, he jerked his finger sharply back and forth, pointing it at me with each word.

I saluted him and said, "Yes, Sir." That was the last order I ever received from any Army officer, even up to a General.

When I graduated as a Second Lieutenant in February 1945, I had received 19 demerits. I wondered why I was allowed to continue in OCS with more than 10 demerits, when everyone else was kicked out.

Second Lieutenant George Frese

Here are the officers that started OCS with me.
I am the second man on the right in the second row from the bottom.

Here are the officers that graduated from OCS with me.
I am the third from the right in the first row.

At graduation, each officer was given his assignment. They went to a Division, a Battalion, a Company, or a smaller group. But there was no assignment for me. And so I was sent to a radio school at Fort Monmouth. I had graduated from Washington State University with a degree in Electrical Engineering and was a licensed Professional Electrical Engineer. Radio school seemed like a logical place for me to be sent, although I already knew what I was being taught. Upon graduating the radio school, everyone in the class was given his assignment. But there was still no assignment for me. So I attended another radio school. This was repeated three or four times. Finally I had exhausted all the radio schools, but I still had no assignment. Why was that?

Then I finally got an assignment. My job was to establish a 40 Kilowatt, multi-channel teletype communication system in the Philippines and to train the team who would operate it. No officer was above me. This put me in charge of all Military communications in the Philippines. I had a group of Privates and Non-Commissioned officers working under me. I worked on this assignment for about a week. I had just gotten acquainted with the men and began explaining the work ahead of us. At this time, the Chief Signal officer in Washington, D.C. reviewed my assignment and canceled it. He said I was not qualified because this position required an officer with the rank of Major or higher. I was only a Second Lieutenant.

The General at Fort Monmouth, New Jersey, then said that he had an even more appropriate assignment for me. I was assigned as the officer in charge of installing new psychological medium and short wave propaganda broadcast radio stations in the Pacific Ocean Area, all beamed at Japan. It was an effort to counteract the negative affect that *Tokyo Rose* was having on our boys. *Tokyo Rose* was a propaganda broadcast of a woman's voice by Japan designed to demoralize our sailors who were stationed on ships in the Pacific Ocean. This was exactly what I was qualified for, and I really wanted to do this job. It was the perfect job for me, and I was thrilled to have this opportunity to develop this broadcast system. I set to work immediately, gathering maps of the Pacific Ocean area showing all of the Pacific islands, compiling a list of manufacturers of medium and short wave broadcast transmitters, and then I was ready to start designing the radio stations. I had no officer over me, and no Enlisted Men (EMs) assigned to me, but I had this great project to do. But then, the same Chief Signal officer in Washington, D.C. saw the assignment, and boom! The assignment was canceled after only a week. He said that this job required a full Colonel and I was only a Second Lieutenant. That Chief Signal officer must have wondered, "Who is this Second Lieutenant who is being given these assignments?"

Since these two assignments were canceled, neither one was placed in my permanent record.

The General at Fort Monmouth then said, "We do not know what to do with you. We have no place to assign you." This is a statement that I heard many times before the end of my military service. How could the army with its vast array of activities not have a single place that they could assign me?

Chapter 2

My First Child

Mollie on the porch
of our apartment

My wife, Mollie, was living off post in an apartment in Ocean Port, New Jersey while I was stationed at Fort Monmouth. She was pregnant and pretty well along. On November 4, 1944 she came on the post, and we did some shopping at the PX (military store on the base). Later that afternoon I walked her to the gate where we parted. That evening, while she was walking home, her water broke. She turned around and walked back to the base hospital.

The next day I was sent to the firing range for target practice. It was cold and rainy. I laid on the ground all day shooting at targets. By evening, I was very cold and developed a fever. I walked to the infirmary and checked in. The next morning when I woke up, the Sergeant asked me if I was related to the lady in the next room who just had a baby. He told me her name was Mollie. Joan Lee was born to us on November 5, 1944.

Joan 3 weeks old

Our family while George in OCS

The Frese family in November of 1944

Chapter 3
War in Europe Ends
Summer to Christmas 1945

The war in Europe ended on May 7, 1945, when Germany surrendered. During the summer and fall of 1945 I was given little things to do which didn't make much sense to me. I was sent to the rifle range or the pistol range for target practice. I was on clean-up detail over and over again. I attended training classes that I had already gone through in Basic Training and some more advanced classes. Occasionally, I got a more interesting task like repairing a motor generator and other electrical jobs. None of the tasks I did during this period ended up in my permanent record, nor did the fact that I was at Fort Monmouth doing anything get placed in my record.

After several months of rather insignificant tasks, the officer at Fort Monmouth said to me, "We have no assignments for you here in the States, so we are going to send you overseas. They will know what to do with you." I had my doubts, but I hoped that in Europe they would have something for me to do.

Before I left for Europe, I had just enough time to move my wife, who was now five months pregnant, and my daughter back home to Spokane, Washington, and be with them for Christmas, December 24 and 25. Before I left Fort Monmouth, they gave me my overseas shots all at once because of the quick timeline for my departure. Boy, that made me quite ill, and I started the trip to Spokane feeling very badly. It was a cold December day when

Mollie, Joan, and I boarded the train headed for Spokane by way of Chicago. Shortly after leaving New York City, the railroad car's heater steam valve got stuck, and our car got hotter and hotter. Finally, they opened the car windows to cool it down. We were one or two cars behind the steam engine, and the soot from the engine stack began to swirl around in the car. Pretty soon, we were all covered with the black stuff. Baby Joan was crying with black tears rolling down her little cheeks, and we were unable to comfort and quiet her. I still felt very sick and had a fever. Breathing in the soot-filled air only added to our misery.

When we arrived in Chicago, the United Service Organization (USO) was at the train station ready to help us right there on the spot. At the time, the USO was an organization of woman that took care of the needs of military personnel as they passed through their local city. The woman took our dirty, black baby, gave her a bath, and washed her clothes. They gave us shower rooms, took our clothes, and washed and dried them. Everything was ready for us in order to board the train to Spokane on time. As the train got going, my fever broke. We all felt great. Baby Joan was laughing and happy as could be. We arrived in Spokane just before Christmas.

Chapter 4
Fort Benning, Georgia, to Camp Shanks, New York
Transportation Officer

We had a short Christmas vacation before I departed for Fort Benning, Georgia. Why I was sent there when I was headed for Europe, I did not know. I soon found out. I was appointed (this was not an assignment) Transportation officer in charge of transferring 830 newly enlisted black men to Camp Shanks, New York. I was the only officer, and there was only one Sergeant among them. Shortly after the train left the station, a sandwich lunch was served. The kitchen car was in the front of the train, and they decided to serve the rear car first. The EM walked down the aisle with a tray of sandwiches held high over his head. After awhile there came a complaint.

"Lieutenant, Sir, the men are reaching over the top of the tray as it passes by and taking a sandwich.

I thought to myself, "How am I going to stop them?"

The Sergeant who was sitting next to me said, "I'll take care of that for you, Sir."

I replied, "Good, take over Sergeant."

A little later, the calm was broken with a loud "**Yeeaool!**" coming from a couple of cars down the line. I rushed to where the noise came from and found a man holding his bleeding arm. I said, "What happened here, Sergeant?"

"Well you see Sir, when the man reached up over the tray to take a sandwich, I sliced his arm with my knife."

"Oh, my gosh, Sergeant, don't ever do that again!"

"Yes Sir, I will never need to do that again, because they won't do it anymore."

Well he was right, they didn't do that anymore. Nothing more became of that issue. We arrived at Camp Shanks in (almost) one piece. When the train stopped at Camp Shanks, the men disembarked, and an officer met me. We saluted, and then the roll was called. At the end of roll call, the officer said to me, "Lieutenant, there are two men missing. Do you know anything about this?"

I replied, "There were a few stops where it might have been possible to jump out of a window, but that seems unlikely." I was thinking to myself, boy now I'm in trouble.

Finally, the officer said to me, "Well congratulations, Lieutenant. You have the best record for losing the fewest men on this trip." Whew, what a relief, but that good job didn't get into my permanent record either.

Chapter 5
Camp Shanks to La Havre, France

I spent New Year's Eve alone in the officer's quarters at Camp Shanks, New York. I still remember what it feels like to be all alone on a special holiday, where the world around you is celebrating and you are all alone, even if only for a short time. The next morning we boarded the 300 foot ocean liner, the *George Washington*, headed for La Havre, France.

It was January 1, 1946 when we set sail. We were in a convoy of ships and could go no faster than the slowest ship in the group. We had to sail in a zigzag pattern, because the German U-boats were still on the prowl, sinking any ships they could find. I don't know whether they didn't get the information that the war was over, or that their orders were to sink any ship they could before they were sunk themselves. I suspect the latter. The weather was said to be the worst in many years. Frequently we encountered storms with winds up to 100 miles per hour and waves that were 100 feet high. Our ship was either going uphill or downhill, rolling over on its left side or the right side. The trip was a long one, taking more than one and a half months. One morning it was awfully good to hear everything silent with the engines shut down. I looked out the porthole window. I could see the port of La Havre, France, a very welcomed sight.

Chapter 6
La Havre, France
The Cultural Shock

After breakfast, we disembarked and started roaming the streets and parks of La Havre. Early that morning I got my first shock. A young lady was walking toward us on the opposite side of the street. In the middle of the block she stepped off the curb, squatted down, and began to pee. I had never seen that before. Later, I observed on my side of the street, men's and ladies' feet and legs visible below a modesty board. I assume they were sitting on a series of holers, but I never went around the end to look. A holer is an outdoor toilet. A one holer seats one person, a two holer has two seats, and a series is one holer after another.

The second shock came later in a park. Two other soldiers and I entered a restroom for both sexes. Standing in the room was what I thought was a funny looking bird bath. None of us knew what it was. A cleaning lady came in, and one of the GI's said to her, "What is that?"

"That's a bidet."

"What's it for?"

"To clean ones self down here," she said as she pointed to the lower mid part of her body.

"Would you show us how it works?"

"Oh no, I would never do that."

"For a package of cigarettes?"

He gave her a pack, and she sat on the thing, swish-swish, got up and left. She was probably able to buy food for several weeks with those cigarettes. I really felt sorry for her, and somehow I liked her. I assumed that we just got a small glimpse of what life was like in France and most of Europe during the war. This woman was willing compromise her dignity and self respect for what a package of cigarettes would bring her and her family.

Chapter 7
Marburg Staging Center

The next morning we were loaded into a train, I think about five cars long, and headed to Marburg, Germany. The cars were made-over box cars. There were wooden seats, some with padding, and glass in some of the windows. It was cold outside, and there was no heat in the cars. The maximum speed was about ten miles per hour, but it usually averaged five, if we were moving at all. The train stopped for several reasons: side tracked to let another train go by, for track repairs, or for meals. The meals were served at track side kitchens. We lined up outside for the mess (army term for meals). The Sergeant slopped the mess into our mess gear. We sat in the cold, anyplace we could find, and ate our meal. When we were through eating, we dipped our mess gear in a large barrel of boiling water. Only it wasn't boiling. I doubt the water ever got over 120°. With the freezing weather, and all the gear going into the barrel, no fire could have kept the water anywhere near boiling. I noticed that my mess gear was not getting clean, so I found paper towels or Kleenex and rubbed and rubbed my gear until it was polished very clean. I think that prevented me from getting sick. Many of the men on the train had diarrhea and were frantically looking for places to go (some managed to jump off and back on the train, while others hung their butts out the window).

As the train traveled at its usual speed, five miles per hour, the men spent their time in a variety of ways. Some would run by the train to keep warm. Some would try to sleep.

As we traveled through the countryside, I could see houses off in the distance. Some of the houses had open windows with laundry draped over the window sill. It must have been awfully cold in those houses. There was no fuel in the area, and I doubt they had much food. I didn't see how they could survive, and I imagine quite a few of them did not.

Finally, after six days of travel we arrived in Marburg. This was the reception center for American Forces entering into Europe. I was given a nice room and told that I would be there only a few days. After several days, all who had arrived with me were gone. Finally, after about a week in Marburg I was called in and they said, "We do not know where to assign you. We have no place to put you here in Europe."

Portion of map I used in Europe
La Havre, France to Marburg, Germany

I said, "You mean to tell me that I was sent to Europe, and you don't have any place to put me."

'No we don't. There is no place that fits what you do.

I did not know what I did. I wondered why there was nothing for me to do. I could train troops. I could do just about anything. Why wouldn't they let me do something?

So, they decided to send me on to Wurzburg, Germany, to the 3110 Signal Corps Company Headquarters. They assured me, that they would know where to place me. "*I doubt that*," was what I thought to myself.

So I was off to Wurzburg, about 100 miles away.

Chapter 8
Signal Corps Battalion Headquarters
No. 3110 Wurzburg, Germany

Just a short daytime train ride and I was in Wurzburg. Looking around after arriving was a shocker. The sky was filled with smoke, and the whole city seemed to be on fire, literally. The day before the war ended, the British Royal Air Force (RAF) had bombed the place to total destruction in just 7 minutes. Wurzburg had been a town of about 150,000 people. The town and its people weren't there now. I arrived in Wurzburg seven months after the war had ended, and the town was still smoldering.

Portion of map I used in Europe
Marburg, Germany, to Wurzburg, Germany

The headquarters for the 3110 Signal Corp Service Battalion was in a large building just south of town. I was given a nice private room with a bathroom down the hall. I waited for a couple of days before they told me that they had nothing for me to do. They did not know what to do with me.

I said "What kind of a special person am I that nobody has anything for me to do, when I am trained to do almost anything; I am a trained officer having been through Officer Candidate School, I know the ropes, and nobody says I can do anything." That had me so puzzled; I just could not understand it. But they assured me that they would come up with a solution.

One aspect of the next few weeks that I was in Wurzburg was actually fun for me. I found a German phonograph player in the dining room. It needed some work, so I fixed it up. This room was used for dances that were held Friday and Saturday nights. Officers would gather some German girls from around the countryside and bring them to dance with the GIs and Officers. I would select and play the records for them.

On the boat ride over from America, I had spent much of my time writing a small booklet on equalizer design, making good use of my slide rule. Now I had the opportunity to practice my design. I found some radio parts, and in the daytime I built audio equalizers to boost the bass and highs. The music sounded so much better and the dancers appreciated the improved sound. I still have that booklet to this day, and it still is a pretty good book.

During the evening dances, some of the men would take a girl up to their rooms. If a girl did not give the guy what he wanted, she would soon appear back downstairs on the dance floor, alone. It became my job to take them home. I felt sorry for these girls and was happy to help them home. They were very pleasant and appreciative of me. My two years of high school

German came in handy. Sometimes upon arriving at a house, the young lady I was driving home would invite me in. I always politely refused, because I did not want any involvement since I was married, and I was somewhat fearful of the unknown, not knowing if one of the girls might have a boyfriend or brother waiting inside who might like to kill an American officer. I realized now that my fears were probably completely unfounded.

During the daytime, I would wander around Wurzburg. It was very badly damaged. At that point, there were no men in the town, only women who really did not have any place to go. There was not much food. What an awful situation for those who survived the bombing. I walked around the streets. I was a little bit leery, so, I carried a carbine in order to look like a soldier who meant business. No one knew that I felt that it was a joke for me to be carrying a gun. I talked to some of the women for a while until it made me feel like crying, because their living conditions made their lives such a struggle. Then I would go on and talk to another one. So I spent my days wandering around Wurzburg, which made me very sad.

A few weeks went by and nothing much was happening in terms of my receiving an assignment. So I went to the office and asked if they could give me something to do. Anything, even training men in close order drill.

"We can't do that Lieutenant, but there is something you may be able to do for us. We would really like you to do this for us. But you have to do it strictly on a volunteer basis. We cannot assign you to it as an official assignment, and we cannot attach you to the battalion. You do not have to do this if you do not want to. You would be just volunteering. It is not an assignment."

"I'll do anything at this point."

"Would you like to go to Berlin and be in charge of all long lines telephone and radio communication in and out of Berlin? There are 4 wire long lines running throughout Germany to Frankfort, Paris, Warsaw, and Moscow. But you only have to do this if you would like to."

I thought, "If I would like to. What kind of a situation am I in that the Army asks me to do an assignment only if I would like to do it? I am just a Second Lieutenant. Why doesn't anyone have authority to send me anywhere?"

Did I hear that right? Do they really want me to be in charge of the whole communication system? I thought I was ready and willing to do anything. But I was taken aback by this offer. Let me think about it. I thought about it for about five seconds and said "I'll do it." At this point, I really was willing try anything.

"Good, we'll get you started for your trip through the Russian sector right away."

I was really perplexed as to what was going on and what to expect next. I was finally asked if I would do something, but I had to volunteer to do it. Why wouldn't the commander at Wurzburg assign me the job? Why in the Army did I have to volunteer in order to do a job? It did feel good to have a job to do after more than a year of incidental activity.

The reason I was taken aback by this offer was that I did not have the qualifications needed for this assignment. I was a broadcast engineer not a long lines telephone expert. When I was in college I worked for the radio station KWSC as Transmitter Operator. My career goal was to become the Chief Engineer for a radio station. When the Chief Engineer at KWSC left, I was offered the position. I was surprised by the offer since I did not feel that I was qualified for this position, but I had the confidence in myself that I would be able to do the things required, so I took the job. I was surprised at how my keen desire to do that job had enabled me to learn the job and do it well. Now, even though I did not know much about operating a telephone communication system, my experience at the radio station gave me the confidence that I would be able to it.

Chapter 9

On to Berlin

The next morning two other men and I left Wurzburg in a truck headed for Berlin, a distance of approximately 325 miles. Our trip went through the Russian Zone (the section of Germany that was occupied by the Russians). Our first stop was at the border of the Russian Zone. The gate guard stopped our truck and asked for our passports. I gave him mine and noticed that he was holding it upside down. He examined it and after a minute or so, he handed it back to me and said, "Allist ist OK." The first two words were German and the last word was Texan.

Portion of map I used in Europe
Wurzburg, Germany, to Berlin, Germany

The countryside was nice, and the small German towns were quaint and interesting with their narrow streets. There was barely room for three small cars, including parking on either side. The buildings were about three stories tall and all the same height.

Late that afternoon we stopped at a house set up for American soldiers traveling through the Russian Zone. This house was occupied by a mother and her two teenage daughters. They had cooked and prepared a meal: meat, mashed potatoes and gravy, vegetables, and desserts. That was one of the best meals that I can ever remember eating. It was so much better than Army food. The conversation was most delightful, and my two years of high school German was put to good use again.

The next morning we entered Berlin. It was foggy, and it remained so for almost all of the month of March. Because we came up from south, I thought we were entering Berlin on the south side. Not so. We entered Berlin from the north side. The first thing I saw was a Russian tank monument

First Russian tank in Berlin

mounted on a ten-foot high platform. This was the first tank that entered Berlin. The American tanks arrived first but waited outside of the city for several weeks. This was done so the Russians could enter Berlin first as per an agreement between the United States and Stalin.

One day in late March I woke up to a sunny day. Oh my, the sun seemed to be rising in the West! I never could get my direction quite straight in my mind. Most of Berlin, as I remember it, is turned around, with the exception of East Berlin. It was, of course, always on the east side of Berlin.

Chapter 10
Settling in Berlin

On arrival in Berlin, I was taken to the 3110 Signal Corps Battalion Headquarters. I was given a private apartment on the third floor with a living room/bedroom/kitchen, bathroom (tub, stove to heat water for bathing, and a toilet), and a closet. I quickly made friends with the maid, and she brought me some real fine furniture from some empty rooms.

My apartment

Looking out my window at the entrance to the
complex where my apartment was located

Outside my window at night

My car

View from the roof of my apartment building
Bombed out buildings were all around

View from the roof of my apartment building
Bombed out buildings were all around

View from the roof of my apartment building
Bombed out buildings were all around

I inherited a group of seven enlisted men (boys really), six Privates and one Sergeant named Harsh, who all worked with telephone communications. However, because they were not officially assigned to me, my care for these boys was not noted in my permanent record. Every man had his own apartment. My responsibility was to oversee the "boys" as their officer. I really

Sergeant Harsh

liked these boys; they were all fine and happy. Each had his own hobby. Some boys collected stamps, others did photography, and there were even those that collected unusual German articles.

Gas station for the Signal Corp

One day, the boys found a wrecked and abandoned jeep. They it brought into the Battalion service station where they were allowed to get it running and even fill it with gas. The boys had a high old time roaming Berlin and finding things for their hobby collections.

About four months later,

there was a turn for the worse for these boys. When I first arrived in Berlin, the Major who should have been above me had gone home. Now his replacement finally arrived. So now I had a Major over me (but not really, because I was just a volunteer for this assignment). He inspected all of the boy's rooms and then told me, "Lieutenant Frese, you tell the boys to throw out all of their junk they have collected, straighten up their room, make their beds, and see that they are properly dressed."

"Sir, I will not do that."

He snapped back, "Lieutenant, I can have you court-martialed for that."

"Sir, I hope you won't do that, but that is your choice." I never saw the Major again.

The "boys"
Amadon, Waters, Nauman, Harse, Clark, Mitchel, Bennett

Some time later the boys came to me and said, "A Major came to us and told us to throw out all our junk. Do we have to do that?"

"Boys, that is up to you. I will not order you to do that. I told the Major that I would not tell you to clean up your rooms and dress properly. He threatened me with a court-martial, but I haven't heard from him since. You boys have to decide what you will do. But if you don't do what he asked, I would expect he will court-martial you."

Sometime later I ran into some of the boys. They reported that things were not good. They cleaned up their rooms and lost their hobbies that had occupied their spare time. Now they were entertaining themselves with other activities. Some were in trouble by getting German girls pregnant. Others were getting into all kinds of mischief. I was so sorry to hear about it. That is all I know about what happened to these boys.

The "boys" on the roof of a building

Chapter 11

Working in Berlin

In Charge of Communications

Farnamt policeman

A short time after I arrived in Berlin, I was taken to Berlin's main telephone Building (the Farnamt Building). This was my base of operation for the next four months, from March through June. There I was introduced to Master Sergeant Dalzell, the only American officer left in the communications center. President Truman had issued an order that all military men who had served more than four years could go home. The Major and the first Lieutenant who had been in charge of the long lines communications had already left. Dalzell was waiting for his replacement, which was me. As soon as I showed up, he was gone.

Dalzell was a professional telephone engineer from Los Angeles. He really knew telephone systems. I only knew the bare essentials about four wire duplex telephone transmission system, and a few smattering bits of other information. The only training Dalzell gave me was to introduce me to two German ladies; Elsie, my secretary, and Marie, the toll test operator. These ladies helped run the German telephone system during the war, and they were an important part of operating it now. After the introductions, Dalzell said, "It's all yours, I'm going home." He was out of there.

Elsie, Marie, and I kept the long lines communications system operating smoothly. I showed great respect for these ladies, would compliment them, and made the time we worked together fun. When a problem arose, Elsie or Marie would bring it to me and explain the issue. I would ask them how they thought it should be solved since they knew far more about how the communication

My desk at work

system operated than I did. After listening to their solution, I would say, "Good, let's do that." There was only one piece of equipment in the whole system that I knew anything about. I was able to repair it one time when it had a problem.

The telephone lines in Berlin had been buried deep underground so that many of them were not damaged by the bombing of Berlin. Therefore many of the remaining buildings still had telephone service.

Elsie and Marie played an important part in American history by providing an invaluable service, badly needed at a critical time for the United States, because they really ran the show for me. Elsie received orders from
Page 40

Battalion Headquarters in Wurzburg and gave them to me to execute. Here is how I executed an order; I gave it to Marie, then asked in German, "Kann Wir Machen iunes Fraulein Marie?" (Can we do that. Miss Marie?)

Toll Test operator - Marie

An order came in that we needed to set up telephone circuits so that the leaders of the United States and Russia (Truman and Stalin) could talk person-to-person. Marie set up the four-wire long lines circuits from Frankfort to Moscow. When the time came for the private conference between President Truman and Joseph Stalin, the call went as scheduled without a hitch. There were two of these calls, as I recall.

Toll Test switchboard

No one was to listen in on these private conversations, except Marie, and she was instructed to just listen in every so often for a bit of time to make sure that the circuit was going well. Nevertheless, I could glean from watching her that things were not going well between the two leaders. I talked with her later, and she confirmed that the talks between the two men were not going well. Truman and Stalin could not come to any agreement as to what should be done with Berlin. The communication between them was further complicated by the need for interpreters.

Elsie Powell, my secretary

Elsie was the younger of the two women. I guess Elsie was between 24 and 28 years of age. She spoke English fluently and was well organized. She was outgoing and lively, fun to be with, had a great sense of humor, and quite attractive.

To get into our work area from the outside, it was necessary to walk through a long, dark hallway. The lights had been shot out by the Russians a few months before and had still not been replaced. One morning as I was entering the building, I heard Elsie coming in behind me. Being a jokester, I pressed myself against the dark wall and as she was walking by me I said (in a rather low soft voice) "boo." My intention was not to scare her too badly. She let out a scream that scared the wits out of me. We both instinctively grabbed each other and she was breathing quite heavily. She said "Oh Lieutenant, you scared me something awful. When she finally calmed down, I apologized, as I did not mean to scare so. And after that we laughed about it. A few days later, I was going through the same hallway, when Elsie let out a loud, "**BOOO.**" That scared me out of my wits and set me off. I screamed and we had about the same immediate reactions as before. After that, we always called out as we entered the hallway. "Are you down there?" Neither one of us wanted to be caught off guard again. That set the stage for more good fun between us, but a little milder as time went on.

Marie was probably around 34 to 38 years old and a very efficient, devoted, and loyal woman. She was a serious business lady and knew how to do her job well. Here is the story I remember most about her. I was in the employee's lounge one morning, when in walked Marie. She stood there for a few seconds, then walked over to me and put her arms around me tightly. This seemed like a rather strange thing for a German woman to do to an American officer. Then she started to cry a little and said, "Lieutenant, you are the only man who has ever treated me so nice." I do not remember my response, but I hope it was appropriate. Then she held me a little tighter and she started to cry. I tried to hold her just as tight as she held me, but no tighter. I used that for my adjustment clue for how I should respond, since I did not yet understand why she was so emotional. She couldn't say anything for a little while, and then she started to tell me her story.

Some months ago, the Russians came barging into the Farnamt Building on a rampage, shooting at anything and anyone in sight. The Russian soldiers rounded up all the women including Elsie and Marie and took them up to the sixth floor. They took them one by one to the roof and threw them off. They laughed and laughed as each girl screamed and splattered on the pavement below. Elsie and Marie were able to hide under a table with the table cloth pulled to the floor. The Russians never found them.

As Marie was telling me this story, something snapped inside me, my emotions took over, and I started to cry. We stood there crying our eyes out for quite a while, holding onto each other, until finally our crying subsided. Without saying a word we slowly departed. I don't remember that we ever said anything about her story again.

The Russians were allowed to enter the city of Berlin first, even though the Americans tanks were there three weeks earlier. The United States allowed the Russians to enter first because of the way the Germans had invaded Russia and mistreated the Russian people. The Russians soldiers were given free rein to do with the civilians whatever they wanted. The soldiers were very angry with the German people. Marie's story touched me deeply when she told me what the Russian soldiers had done to them. Even today, it still has a deep emotional impact when I think about it. If I tell anyone about this story, the emotions that I felt then well up inside of me, and I struggle to hold the tears back.

Signal Corp switching equipment

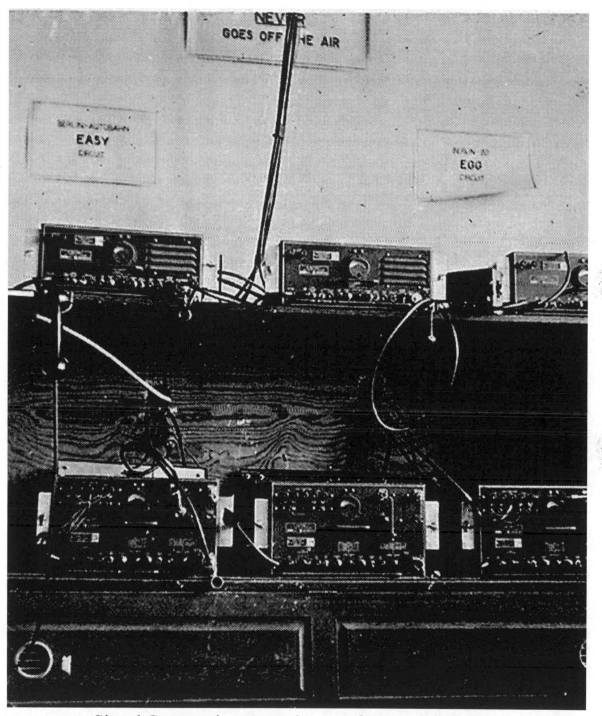

Signal Corp equipment at the top of Farnamt building

A Private in charge of signal equipment in Farnamt building

Chapter 12

Afternoon Tea

In addition to the American communications operation, the Farnamt Building was also the location of the English and the French communications operations. Every afternoon at 3:00 o'clock, an officer from the French operation and I were invited to tea by an officer from the English operation. I always attended this afternoon tea, but because I don't like tea, I always politely refused the tea. After two or three weeks of attending these afternoon teas, the French officer came to me and said, "George, do you know that you are causing an international incident?"

"No. How could I be doing that?"

"The word is getting around that the American and English communication officers are not getting along."

"How so is that?"

"Because you refuse to drink tea with the English officer. You had better start drinking your tea when it is offered to you."

So at the next tea, I said, "I think I will try some tea. Oh my, this is really good."

To this day, I still do not like tea.

Chapter 13
Activity in the American Sector of Berlin

Looking around in the American sector of Berlin, it was obvious that German women were working everywhere. There were no men. They were all killed in the war. The women were given jobs cleaning up the piles and piles of rubble created by the bombing. The women passed the bricks from one woman to another until they reached a place where another group of women scraped the mortar off the bricks so they could be used to rebuild Berlin. All women were paid the same, no matter what they did. For example, the two very skilled women working for me in communications were paid the same amount as common laborers working cleaning up the rubble. That pay was enough money to buy only 980 calories of food a day. It had

Women gathering bricks

been determined that 980 calories was the right amount to keep a woman strong enough to work, but it was not enough food to really satisfy the hunger.

Women passing bricks

Women cleaning bricks

When I realized how hungry Elsie and Marie were, I went across the street to the PX (military store) and bought a sack of hamburgers. When I brought them back, they each took their chair, placed the chair in opposite corners of the room facing the wall and began to eat. They used both thumbs to push food into their mouths, until I could see that their cheeks looked like they would burst. I had never seen such hunger. After satisfying their hunger, they both worked even harder for me than before. After that, I brought them a little something extra to eat every day.

Chapter 14

Lost in the Russian Sector

A Very Scary Story

One day, I decided I wanted to visit East Berlin to see what it was like. At this time East Berlin was not walled off from West Berlin, and we were allowed to go into East Berlin. I took off in my truck. There were many roads crossing into East Berlin, and I crossed on one of them. The first thing I noticed was that nothing was going on. For some time I didn't see any people. Finally, I came to a store, and low and behold, someone was going in. I decided to go in and have a look. Inside there were rows and rows of empty shelves. Then I spotted in one corner some loaves of bread. The lady that went in ahead of me bought a loaf of bread. Bread was very cheap, but people apparently didn't have much money.

As I drove on, a deep fog rolled in. Soon I realized that I was lost. I didn't know where I was going; north, south, east, or west, or in circles. I slowly drove on. Then before me appeared two Russian soldiers motioning me to get out of the car and follow them. They led me into a complex where there was a Russian officer, and two German men. There were now four of us in the room: the Russian officer, a Russian to German interpreter, a German to English interpreter, and me. Apparently in the fog, I had driven into a Russian Compound and had not seen any signs that may have been there to tell me to keep out.

The Russian officer asked me through the interpreters, "What are you doing here in East Berlin?"

"I am sightseeing," I replied back up though the interpreters.

"So, you do admit that you were spying."

"No, I am not a spy." I am thinking about what to say to get out of this mess. Every attempt, to rephrase my answer, failed to convince the Russian officer that I was only sightseeing.

Finally, the Russian officer said, "Here is what you are to do. Get in your car and head back to West Berlin as quickly as you can."

I was not sure what that really meant. Did it mean for me to go fast, as if I were trying to escape, so that they would have an excuse to shoot me, or were they trying to get me out of East Berlin? I had no choice but to do what he said. I drove pretty fast, but not too fast. Finally, I realized that I was not going to be shot because I was out of range and in the fog.

Now I faced my original problem. I didn't have the slightest idea where I was, and I couldn't see where I was going. I stopped to think. I couldn't keep driving, or I might have wound up in Warsaw, Poland. I sat still maybe half an hour. Suddenly, I saw a little hole, like a donut hole, opening up in front of me. The hole tunneled deep into the fog. I saw the steeple of a church way in the distance. I recognized what it was. It was the top cone of the German Lutheran Church in the American section in West Berlin. Half of the cone was blown off, split vertically down the middle. That church with its half-cone spire is still there today, as a monument of World War II.

Now that I knew which way was west, I began to drive very slowly. I was trying to keep track of how much I turned to the right and then to the left.

German Lutheran church

After what seemed to me a long time, I felt I was getting nowhere, that I no longer knew my direction. So I parked to wait until the fog lifted and thought about what to do next. It is a terrible feeling to be lost, particularly when you might be in a situation that could endanger your life.

As I was sitting there gazing out my left side window, I noticed some church steps. I looked up, and there, at the top, was the German Lutheran Church Spire, the one with the half-cone blown off. What a feeling of relief came over me! Now I knew where I was, fog or no fog, in West Berlin! Boy oh boy, was I glad to get back to my apartment that day.

Chapter 15
Berlin Black Market
Another Scary Story

The black market in Berlin was a well known area. Most people do not have any idea how the black market functioned. I decided to go into the area to see how it worked. It was a large open space, about 4 or 5 acres or so with no buildings. There were lots of people just milling around, walking very slow, seemingly going no place. I decided I would join in and see if I could find out what they were doing.

As I walked past a person, I observed that he would say something in a few words. Sometimes he spoke in German, sometimes in English. As I listened closer, I heard that he was peddling something such as silk stockings, tableware, cameras, stamp collections, just about everything. Whatever they were peddling was what they had in their back pack. Once again, my high school German came in handy.

I walked past a man as he said, "A camera."

I replied, "How much?"

"Two packs of cigarettes."

"I'll take it."

And he reached into his pack and pulled out a camera and I gave him the two packs. Cigarettes were the medium of exchange. Money was not worth anything at the black market. I also brought some silk stockings for my wife, a pair of binoculars, and a few other items.

Later, I decided it would be fun to go back into the black market area and take some pictures so the people back home could see what the black market area looked like. Back at the market, I found a high spot overlooking the area. From that location, I began to focus in on some areas. Before I took any pictures, I looked up, and I saw on my right side three Russian officers rapidly nudging their way through the crowd headed right toward me. Then I looked to my left side and saw three more Russian officers, also headed in the same manner toward me. I did not know why they were coming at me, but I sensed that this was not good. Fortunately, my car was parked out on the street headed in the direction I needed to go to get out of there. I left my high spot and ran through the crowd even faster than the Russians that were coming after me. I got into my car and left quickly. Looking back, I saw them standing on the street watching me leave. I was glad to escape out of there!

Back home, having dinner with my officer friends, I told them of my afternoon experience. An officer explained to me, "You are really lucky that you got away. Russian law demands that any Russian officer caught in the black market be shot. They go into the black market anyway. Because you were taking pictures, they were afraid that could get them killed. They would have killed you on the spot if they caught you."

I never went back to the black market.

Chapter 16
Taking Pictures around Berlin

Taking a picture of myself in a mirror

With that Rolacord camera, I took several hundred pictures until my discharge from the Army. I wanted to share with my family the things that I experienced while I was in Germany.

Taking a picture of the French monument in Berlin

French monument

Allies monument

One of the places that I saw as I toured around West Berlin was Hitler's underground headquarters. He had moved his headquarters from the government buildings to this underground location in the later days of the war, when the war was no longer going well for Germany. I went inside and down the stairs to where his office was. The place was pretty well destroyed, most likely by the Russians when they entered Berlin. There was nothing much to see. I don't recall any furniture. The ceilings had holes open to the outdoors, and many of the walls were badly damaged. This is where Hitler and Eva Braun, his girl friend, committed suicide by taking cyanide. Their bodies were burned at the entrance to his headquarters, and the ashes from the fire were still on the ground.

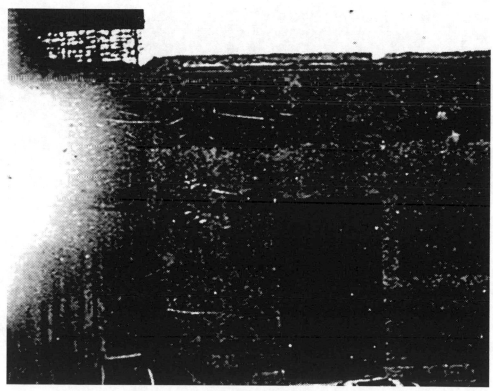

Hitler committed suicide here

Hitler's office

Hitler's headquarters

In the foreground of this picture is where Hitler's and Eva's bodies were burned after they committed suicide. The ash from the fire was still on the ground.

I also went to the Templehof Airport. All around the runway, as far as the eye could see, were smashed up airplanes. These planes had made it back from their missions, but were no longer able to fly. So they had taken a bulldozer and pushed them off to the side of the runway. There were hundreds, maybe up to a thousand of these planes just sitting there. No effort had yet been made to clean up this area.

War damaged planes beside the airport runway

War damaged planes beside the airport runway

Chapter 17
Climbing the World's Tallest Tower

In 1946, the world's tallest television tower was located in Berlin. It was 518 feet tall, with Berlin's first television station at the top.

Television tower

When the Russians came into Berlin, they shot it up, producing extensive damage to the whole structure. The elevator shaft was missing. Large sections of the stairs were missing. The only way to get up to the top of the tower was to climb the exposed metal structure one of the tower's three support legs.

Looking straight up the TV tower at the damaged elevator shaft

Looking straight up from the base

Three of us hams (amateur ham radio operators), Bud Spalding, Bill Keller, and I decided to climb the tower to see the sights and see what was up there. Bud scampered up the tower like he had been a tower worker. I wasn't afraid, but I took it slow and easy. Bill was really scared. Bud got to the top first, I was second, and Bill arrived sometime later.

Bud on the way up tower

When I was almost to the top, Bud yelled down to me saying, "Take a picture of me." When I looked up, I saw Bud standing on the outer edge of the ground plain antenna. This plain antenna was made of heavy pipe. The ground plain was a horizontal circle with a radius of about 40 feet. Bud was standing out there at the end of this pipe, 550 feet above the ground.

I was carrying my camera on a strap over my shoulder. I was hanging on the tower with my left hand, and with my right hand trying to get the camera into place so that I could take a picture. Aiming straight up, focusing, and clicking with one hand was a real challenge. I did get the picture. However, Bud was tired of waiting and was on his way back, so he was no longer at the very end when I snapped it.

Bud Spalding on the antenna at the top of the tower

When I got to the top Bud was waiting for me. After quite a while Bill finally arrived. It was evident that he was scared, but he was determined he was going to do it. Notice that his eyes are closed in this picture. What is not visible in this picture is how much Bill was shaking.

Bill and I on top of the TV tower

On the top of the tower, the 40 MHz antenna was intact. There were 120 copper wires running out to the heavy pipe structure that Bud had been standing on. This is the same standard ground system used by broadcast stations in the United States. We looked for the TV transmitter room but found none. Our conclusion was that it was mounted on the underside of the roof we were standing on.

Bud scampered down the tower first. Climbing down was a problem for me. It was difficult to find a foot support, and I had to make sure each foot was secure before I shifted my weight onto the next one. When I got down, it felt so good to be on the ground! I am sure that Bill felt the same way.

Bud and Bill at the base of the tower

The view of Berlin from the top of the tower was well worth the effort it took to get there, and I took several pictures. In the near distance was a race track where sports cars raced at speeds over 100 miles per hour.

Race track from the top of the tower

After we got down from the tower, we went to the track and tried it with our jeep. The jeep could not get above 60 mph. At this speed, we could barely get up on the slope of the curve, much less up the 100 MPH vertical wall.

60 mph on the race track

Chapter 18
Suzette is Born

On April 25, 1946, Suzette Ann was born in Spokane, Washington. My wife, Mollie, sent me word by telegram. The telegraph office was directly across the street from the Farnamt Building. However, the telegram was not delivered until a week after it arrived.

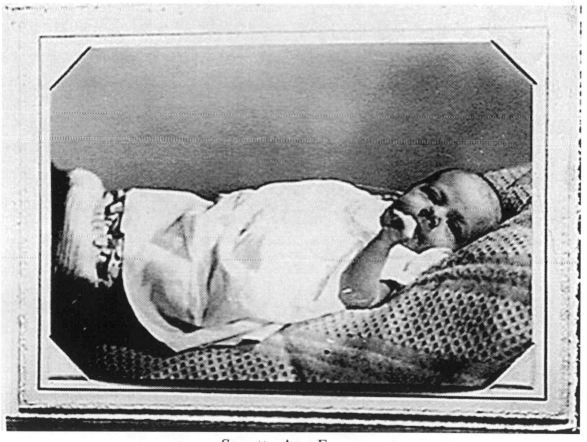

Suzette Ann Frese

Joan, Mollie, and Suzette
Joan is one and a half years old.
Suzette is three weeks old.

When Elsie and Marie found out, they went out and got a vase of flowers for me.

Flowers from my staff

In this picture I am standing in front of the Farnamt Building. Notice the pock mark holes in the building which were the result of the Russians shooting at anything when they first entered Berlin.

Chapter 19

New Replacements Arrive

My replacement

President Truman sent replacements to Europe and gave the order that any man that had served four years in Europe could go home if he wanted to. I had only been in Europe six months, so that surely did not include me, in as much as I had 18 months more to serve. The 3110 Signal Corps Battalion received a professional long lines telephone officer, so they sent him to Berlin to replace me.

The Battalion officer in Berlin said to me, "George, you are free to do whatever you want to do. You are welcome to keep your Berlin apartment and dine with us if you wish, or go do whatever you want to do while finishing your term here in Europe." No assignment for me. I was free to do whatever I wanted to do. Was I really in the Army?

Page 76

I decided to stay in Berlin. I was familiar with Berlin and what else could I really do anyway? Since broadcast engineering was my life love, I decided I would go over to the American Forces Network (AFN) which was a broadcast radio station, and see if they could use me. I told the Major (who was the station manager) of my qualifications as a Professional Radio Broadcast

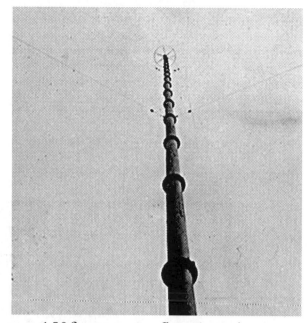

150ft antenna - first American broadcast antenna in Berlin

Engineer, that I could speak some German, I had an apartment here in Berlin and nothing to do. The Major was absolutely delighted to have me come to work with the AFN because they were installing a new radio broadcast station. This is another instance where I was available for a specific task at the right time. Who else but me had the technical background in radio broadcasting in Berlin at that time who could have directed this project?

Two top German Scientists who were Broadcast Engineers, Reichart and John, had been assigned to work for the American Forces Network and to assemble a radio station to broadcast to the American troops. I would guess that these men were around 45 to 50 years old. Even though I was just a kid out of college, these two men discerned that I knew a great deal about radio broadcasting, and they had nothing but respect for me, and I for them. They had not been in the German military during the war because they were highly respected in their field and had, among other accomplishments, designed and built radio stations and the German tank radios. But these scientists were somewhat helpless without an American officer to direct them on this project. The Signal Corps had sent a 1KW Dorehty class B Linear Transmitter to use for this radio station. The German scientists had never

Reichart – German scientist and friend

seen a transmitter like this. To make matters worse, some critical key parts in the output loading circuit were missing. Without my help, the radio station may never have been assembled. I was very familiar with the transmitter, so I recognized that parts were missing. But how to get the transmitter assembled without these critical parts was a dilemma. The two German scientists and I came up with some very innovative modifications. Together, we decided to convert the present transmitter over to a high level Class B Modulation System. We all understood how that type of system worked.

But to convert transmitter we had to high level Class B Modulation System required a large, heavy modulation transformer. "Where could we possibly get one?" I wondered. To my amazement, Reichart said that he had this critical part. It was about 2:00 am in the morning. We got a cart, went

Page 78

down the street a couple of blocks and crawled through a space in the rubble, where his wife was sleeping. He woke her up, reached under the bed, and pulled out the transformer that we needed. He and his wife were living in the rubble of a bombed out building.

We loaded the transformer onto the cart and took it back to the station. These scientists had the foresight to hide the good radio parts so that when the time came that they needed them, the parts were available. They did this because they loved their work and their transmitter more than whichever country might be occupying them at the time. When the American forces were approaching the city where their broadcast station was located, they took apart the transmitter and hid all the critical parts so that they would not be damaged by the fighting. After the Americans took the city, they put the transmitter back together for the Americans to use. When it was apparent that the German army was going to retake the city, they again took apart the transmitter and hid all the parts. Then they put the transmitter back together when the Germans were there. They did this cycle one more time when the Americans retook the city again.

We rearranged and mounted all the parts, overcame several obstacles, finished the construction, and turned on the transmitter. After a few adjustments, it was working very well. Our transmitter became the first 1 KW American Forces Network transmitter in Berlin.

Transmitter under construction

Finished transmitter

One night around midnight, some German women came into where we were working. They had hamburgers and beer to give us boys a break. I told one of the women that I didn't drink beer and ask her if she had coke. She replied, "yes," and brought me one. We started to eat our hamburgers, and soon I reached for my coke. I noticed that my two German scientist friends were not drinking their beer.

I asked them, "What's the matter? I thought you liked beer?"

"Oh! We love beer."

"Then why are you not drinking your beer?"

"The Lieutenant don't drink beer, we don't drink beer."

All at once, I got it, so I said, "If you men do not drink your beer, then I cannot drink my coke, and I *love* my coke!"

They looked at each other, started up with a little "ha," then a "ha-ha," then "ha-ha-ha," and finally they just burst into laughter. They began to sing, grabbed the beer mugs, clinked them together, drank up, and had a high old time. I finished my coke, and we were a happy bunch of men.

Chapter 20
Amateur Radio

Amateur radio has had a great influence on my entire life, from about 10 years of age until the present. My first call sign was W7FMI. My second call was D4AJD (a German call sign). In Berlin, if you had an American amateur radio license, all you needed to

German amateur license

do to get a German license was to apply for it. You did not have to pass a test.

Amateur radio club meeting I am chairing

My present call is AA7H. Not only did amateur radio play a very significant part in my life, but Amateur radio also played a large part during World War II. However, for the Germans, the part it played was negative.

Newspaper picture about our meeting

Berlin D4s, QSO!

American radio "hams" got together last Sunday at AFN Berlin to talk over common problems and discuss their new organizational set-up, tentatively titled American Radio Amateur Hams in Berlin. Left to right: T/3 W E Bosselman, 3160th Sig Sv; RM2c M Glog; T/5 J Batchelder, 3112th Sig Sv; 2nd Lt D Carter, 3110th Sig Sv; 2nd Lt W Keller, 16th Cav Gp; 2nd Lt F C Johnstone, AFN Berlin; 1st Lt A J Hannum, 3112th Sig Sv; 2nd Lt V G Spaulding, AFN Berlin; 2nd Lt R W Weise, 3110th Sig Sv; 2nd Lt G M Frese, 3160th Sig Sv; Aneta Siegel, AFN Berlin; Lt Col A H Green, BD Hq; T/3 W F Block, 78th Sig Co; 2nd Lt C C Busse, ACS Tempelhof; 1st Lt L Friedman, 16th Cav Gp; 2nd Lt W R Triplett, ACS Tempelhof.

Names of the HAMs in attendance

Gill and Benny – English HAMs

All radio began with amateurs. There were no professional radio engineers. It was amateur radio hobbyists who were completely responsible for the early development of radio. They built their own equipment out of whatever parts they could make up to transmit to each other. These amateurs, called HAM radio operators, used their HAM stations to talk to each other all around the world.

While I was wandering around Berlin, I came across an open underground storage warehouse that had lots of parts and equipment. It was the warehouse of the Telefunken Company, a manufacturer of communications equipment. I found German tank radio transmitters and took two of them. I played around with these transmitters and was able to set up an amateur radio station.

Roy's (another HAM) antenna is on the right. Mine is on the left.

I was hoping to be able to talk with my wife back home in Spokane. In the process of working with these FM tank transmitters to set up an AM amateur radio station, I discovered something new about the relationship between AM and FM modulation that was unknown in the United States at that time. I was very excited to demonstrate my new discovery to the German scientists.

Page 86

I was demonstrating my D4AJD amateur radio station to my two German scientist friends (Reichart and John) who were assigned to AFN (American Forces Network). They didn't seem to be very impressed with my amateur station, except that they noticed I was using two of their German FM tank transmitters to make my AM transmitter. Even then, they were not very impressed with my discovery. I really thought that I had found something new and great. But then Reichart explained to me that they used this same system which I had just "discovered" in their 100,000 Watt AM broadcast transmitters which they had built during the war. It was a big letdown for me because I was so excited to discover something unknown only to find out that they already knew about it.

I still wanted to show my friends how my amateur station worked.

I said, "Let me demonstrate for you how it works."

I tuned in a station in Chicago, Illinois using a 10 meter amateur radio band. From the person in Chicago came a general inquiry call, a CQ, which is basically somebody asking "Is there someone listening that would like to talk to me?" I answered the CQ and the W9 came right back to me with a good report stating that I was loud and clear.

Suddenly, there was an explosion of German words back and forth between the two scientists, the likes of which I had never heard and I could not understand. There were speaking so fast and so excitedly back and forth to each other that I could not follow the conversation. They were shocked as they realized that it was their lack of knowledge of 10 meter VHF propagation that was primarily responsible for the Germans' defeat in the war in North Africa. They were shouting in German, "This is why we lost the war in North Africa! It was our fault!" And it really was their fault. They were professional scientists – engineers – and considered amateur radio beneath their dignity. They had never bothered to learn the propagation characteristics of VHF radio which was used by amateurs.

Ten meter VHF propagation was spotty during the German campaign in North Africa from April 1941 through May 1943. Sometimes the communications from the German tanks in Africa could be heard in the Illinois area, but nowhere else. Sometimes they could be heard in Texas, but nowhere else, and so on. Amateur radio operators were located all over the United States. It seems likely that if they heard a message from a German tank commander giving directions for the next tank attack, they called the Army Signal Corps at Fort Monmouth, New Jersey on the land line. From there the message was sent to European Command by the transoceanic cable, and then radioed to the American tank Commander in North Africa. Once the Americans had this information, the American tanks would get to Rommel's (the German tank commander) target area first. Then they would finish off the German tanks as they arrived. Most of this description is conjecture on my part, because I don't know exactly how all the information was relayed from the amateur radio operators to the American tank commanders in North Africa, but this explanation seems to make the most sense to me.

The German scientists knew their tank radios had a broadcast range of line of sight on the ground. As long as the tanks were within sight of each other, they could communicate. What the German scientists and also the German army did not know was that the radio signal was reflected in the atmosphere and could be received around the world. Any amateur radio operator knew this. These scientists were just realizing how the American Forces always knew where the German tanks were located and what Rommel was planning to do with the German tanks. Consequently, the German tanks were defeated in North Africa.

My ten meter amateur radio station
Front view

My amateur radio station transmitter
Back view

Amateur radio station transmitter power supply

My amateur radio antenna

My antenna from Bud Spalding's window

Chapter 21
Orders from Washington
Military Personnel not Needed, May Go Home

Sometime around July of 1946, new orders from Washington to all Battalion and Company headquarters in Europe stated that they could send anyone home who was not needed. Any military personnel could choose to remain in Europe and serve out their original assignment of two years if they wanted to stay.

The officers I ate meals with in the officers' dining room, knew I was just a "volunteer." One of them suggested that I could go home. Since I had no assignment and no one to report to, I decided to see whether this was possible, even though I had only served six months of my two-year term in Europe. The Signal Corps Battalion did not care since my replacement for the long lines communications had arrived. However, the American Forces Network was upset with the idea of my leaving. But since I was not assigned to them, they had no authority do anything about it. As I pondered this suggestion, I thought that maybe, just maybe, I could go home.

But then a big problem developed that prevented me from leaving Berlin. At the end of the war, Germany was divided into four parts. France, England, and the United States each occupied a section in the western part of Germany, while the Russians occupied the eastern part of Germany. Berlin was in the eastern part that was occupied by the Russians. The United States, England, and France all agreed about what to do with Berlin, but the Russians would not agree. The tension got so high in the negotiations that the Russians put a blockade around Berlin. No trains, planes, or cars were allowed to leave the city. The Stalin-Truman talks had broken down, so Stalin had announced that he was going to blow Berlin off the map. The Russians surrounded the city with large guns and were ready to blow it up. This was the first Berlin blockade. It was in July 1946 and was kept top secret because our government did not want the American public to know that the United States and Russia were not getting along at all. Few people back home ever heard of this blockade. The second blockade of Berlin by the Russians is referred to as the Berlin Airlift that occurred from June 1948 to May 1949. This second blockade is well known.

Chapter 22
Risky Chance to Escape Out of Berlin

During an evening meal in the officers' dining room shortly after the blockade started, an officer said that the next day a special train was leaving for Frankfort. It was carrying secret documents. Later that evening, another officer said to me, "George, why don't you get on that train?"

"How can I do that?"

"There is a Master Sergeant taking the tickets as you enter the train, just pull rank."

I had never used my rank as an officer to try to do something, so I was taken aback by this idea.

"Whoa there! How do I do that?"

"Tell him you are on a top secret mission that cannot be disclosed to anyone. You'll get on, trust me."

Chapter 23

Train Ride from Berlin to Frankfort and on to Bremen

Boarding the train to leave Berlin

I walked up to the Master Sergeant who was guarding the doorway to the coach and said, "Sergeant, I am on a top secret mission, and I need to board this train to Frankfort." After pausing for a moment he said, "You may pass." I walked up the steps and onto the train. There were only a few people on the train and nobody said anything to anybody. I was not about to talk with anyone so that my "top secret" mission would remain a secret.

I was very excited at the thought of going home to be with my wife and my daughters, especially to see Suzette for the first time, to be away from the Russian blockade, and to be going back to civilian life.

Since this first Russian blockade of Berlin was kept secret from the public, I do not know how long it lasted, because I left Berlin before the blockade ended.

I cannot explain to you all the feelings and experiences that I had while I was in Europe, and how they shaped the rest of my life. I lived and worked with people from a different culture, and I saw things from a different perspective. It is a big deal for an engineer to see something from a different perspective.

Guns going back to Russia

Very soon the train was on its way. The scenery was not what I had expected. I was sitting on the left side by the window. There was a steady flow of trains going north, headed for Russia. They were loaded with booty taken from German households. There were tables, chairs, beds, mirrors, grandfather clocks, cars, and so on. Then the cargo would shift to tanks and large guns of all types and sizes. Then it was back to more plunder. That is what dominated the scenery most of the way through the Russian sector on the trip to Frankfort.

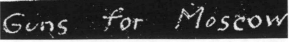

Guns for Moscow

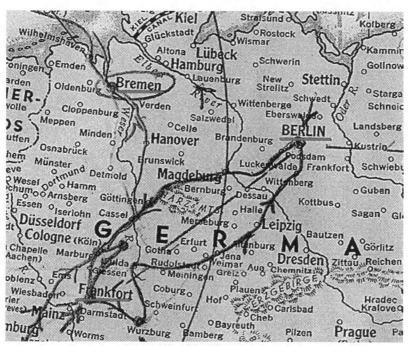

Portion of map I used in Europe
Berlin to Frankfort to Bremen

I arrived at Frankfort and was on my own as to how to get home. I found that U.S. military officers could board trains for free. An officer could just get on and go. So I got on a train headed for Bremen, Germany.

Leaving Frankfort

Train to Bremen

What I remember most vividly about this trip were the children. They ranged from about five to fifteen years of age and gathered around the train wherever we stopped. They were looking for handouts from the soldiers. Candy bars were the most popular thing. I was glad that I had brought some candy bars so that I could share them with these children.

Children at a stop on the way to Bremen

More children meeting the train

Chapter 24
Finance Officer on the George Washington
Going Home

Bremen train station

After arriving in Bremen, I found my way to check in for boarding a troop ship going to the United States. I told them I would like the fastest way to the States. They said that the next boat going to America with an available officer quarters would be leaving in four months. But if I were willing to sleep at the very bottom of the boat, I could be on the next one, the George Washington.

When I checked it out only a few men were down there. I do not remember whether it was the D deck or the G deck, but I do know it was a long way down. Water was on the floor, and it smelled funky. I said, "I'll take it."

Then I was told, "Lieutenant, I have a job for you. I would like to appoint you as the ship's Finance officer." He went on and gave me the details for what I was to do. It seems to me that the only jobs I ever got were the ones where I just happened to come along, and they just happened to have a job that needed to be done, and there was no other officer around to do it but me. None of these volunteer jobs ever made it into my permanent record.

My instructions were to gather up all of the currency control books from each Private and Non-Commissioned officer who was going to be on the George Washington and record the amount of American money each man was allowed to take from Europe. Then I was to go unaccompanied to a designated location, build a fire, and burn all the control books. So, that is what I did. As far as I know, there was no other record of these books.

Before sailing, I went to the bank to get the money to pay these men. I introduced myself as the Finance officer on the USAT George Washington, and I requested the amount of money needed to cover what was owed the men in US currency. I do not remember how much money it was, but it was a very, very large sum, most likely in the millions of dollars. The money was put into

Portion of map I used in Europe
Bremen, Germany to New York City

barracks bags, and I carried all this money into a special room on the ship. I began to put money into an envelope for each man, according to what I had recorded that he was owed from his currency control book. When I finished doling out the money, I was only five cents short. I called each man into my room and gave him his money. I was finished just a few days before we arrived in New York.

Chapter 25
On the George Washington for New York
Continuing on to Fort Lewis

The George Washington

Sometime in mid-July, we left Bremerhaven for New York. The trip was pleasant except for my night quarters. It was a short six or seven day trip, with wonderful sunny summer weather. The time passed very quickly.

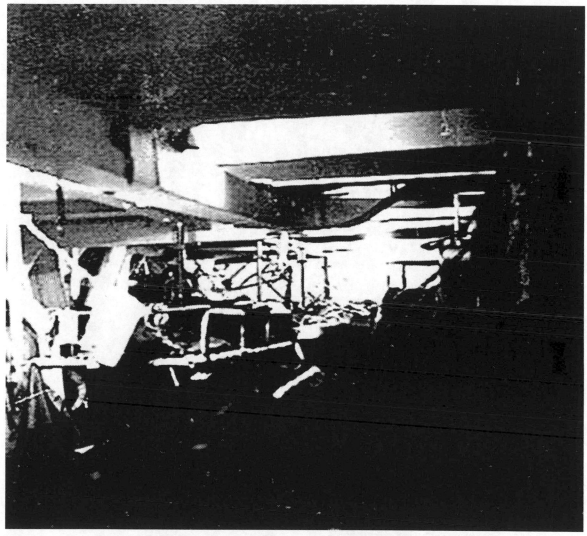

My night quarters on the George

Sunken ships in the English Channel

White cliffs of Dover on the English shoreline

New York City skyline in 1946

Tugboat docking the George Washington in New York

In New York I boarded a troop train headed for Fort Lewis, Washington. The cars on the train were not very nice.

Train from New York to Fort Lewis

After three or four days of travel, I woke up around midnight because the train had stopped. My hay fever, which I had not experienced since I left Washington State, after graduating from Washington State University in Pullman about two years earlier, had now returned in full force. I asked someone, "Where are we?" He replied that we were in Ellensburg, Washington. I should have known. Ellensburg is a farming community at the edge of the Cascade Mountains. The next morning we arrived at Fort Lewis, where I expected it to be a simple matter to get discharged. Boy was I surprised!

Chapter 26

Fort Lewis Discharge Center

Dishonorable Discharge or One to Two Years in the Brig

Inducted in and discharged out at
Fort Lewis, Washington

I arrived at Fort Lewis, Washington in August of 1946 to be discharged from the Army. I walked up to the discharging officer, a Major, and handed him my papers.

He said to me, "What did you do while you were in the Army?"

I said, "Among other things, I was in charge of all the four-wire long lines telephone circuits and radio communications in and out of Berlin during the spring and early summer of this year. I also was in charge of the installation of radio station AFN Berlin. Those were the main things that I did, but I had other little jobs, like running the troops from Fort Benning, Georgia to Camp Shanks, New York. And I was the Finance officer on the George Washington."

The officer looked at me, delayed speaking for a little bit, and then finally said, "You're a liar."

I was taken aback by this.

"How can you say that I am lying?"

"Because your service record is totally blank. It does not show that you ever served in Europe, that you were under the command of any officer, or anywhere else since you graduated from Officer Candidate School. Also, you could not have not been in Europe long enough to be here asking to be discharged. I'll tell you what I am going to do. I'll give you a dishonorable discharge with no severance pay."

"Sir, that is unacceptable to me. I have served my country well during this time of great need."

"In that case, you will stand a court-martial trial, and you will be found guilty not only of being AWOL (absence without official leave) for a considerable length of time, but also for lying to an officer. You will spend at least a year in prison."

I thought about it for a moment and said, "I'd rather be court-martialed. I was not willing to be dishonorably discharged. I knew I was not lying and although nothing was in my service record, I had served, and I knew it could be proven.

The officer was surprised by my decision and said, "I can prove that you are lying, and that will go doubly hard for you."

I told him, "Go ahead and prove it."

He picked up the telephone, and put in a direct call to the General in command of Berlin. "Have you ever heard of a Lieutenant George Frese?"

"Never heard of him," were the words that he repeated from his discussion with the General.

"Well tell me, how did the communications go in and out of Berlin and the rest of Germany, in early spring to summer of this year?" The General told the discharging officer that they went just fine, for had they not gone well his Colonel would have reported it to him.

The officer hung up and said to me, "I cannot prove that you are lying, so here is what I am going to do. I will give you an honorable discharge. But I will not give you the normal increase in rank or any severance pay." I immediately replied that I would accept that. I may be the only Second Lieutenant ever given an honorable discharge without an increase in rank or severance pay. But I was happy that I was not facing a court-martial and a prison sentence, so it felt like a good offer.

I feel certain that the discharging officer did want to send me off to the Brig (the name for the military prison) and then have it proven that I was not lying.

I was glad to be home to join my wife, my daughter Joan, and to meet my new daughter, Suzette, who was now three months old. And now I was able to start my professional career as a radio broadcast engineer.

Epilogue
The Mystery is Still a Mystery

In this book, the history portion is pretty well spelled out. The role that the long lines communication played in setting up the calls between Truman and Stalin, the first Russian blockade of Berlin in the summer of 1946, the contrast between the restoration activity in the American sector and the deserted streets in the Russian section, and other general information about Germany and Berlin at the end of the war are easy to grasp and understand. But the mystery seems to be more obscure. The questions that have remained in my mind since my discharge from the military are these:

1) Why was I from the start of my military service singled out from the rest? I was not sent to the infantry. I was made a Corporal in Basic Training, and the others were Buck Privates. I was not kicked out of Officer Candidate School when I got too many demerits.

2) Why would or could they not assign me to a Battalion, Company, Squad, or small group to do something? This happened over and over again.

3) Why was I not given anything to do except little quickie one shot jobs, for which I was the only available officer for that job and therefore in total charge?

4) Why was I asked if I wanted to *volunteer* for a critically essential job in Berlin? They told me that they could not assign me the job, but it was okay for me to do this job if I wanted to volunteer. I was getting desperate to do anything at all, so I just said okay. Only after I accepted the job was it

described to me. I would be the officer in charge of, and responsible for, all the American radio and long lines telephone communication systems in and out of Berlin to the rest of Germany including Frankfort, and on to Paris, Warsaw, and even to Moscow in Russia. That sounded unreal to me. What was I in for? I know now that they had no other choice but me. All the earlier officers, the Major, First Lieutenant, and Master Sergeant, that were running the communication system before I arrived, were allowed to go home, because they had fulfilled their four years of military service. I was the only possibility that the Signal Corps had of someone who *maybe* could do the job that these three officers had been doing, because there was no other officer in Europe at that time who had the technical knowledge and experience to run the long lines communication system.

As I left for Berlin, I was committed, and I was determined to do this job, and I did it. But as I look back, I wonder how I ever could have done it.

Sixty-five years later and I am still pondering, "How did I do that?" Engineers, by nature, always explore a subject until they find everything they can possibly uncover. That's how new discoveries are made. So when a question arises in the mind of an engineer, it stays there until answers are found.

So this question has remained with me. How was it that I was in Europe with nothing to doing at the moment when there was an unfulfilled need to have someone run the long lines communication systems, and I was able to this job without having the required technical knowledge? At times, I come up with little ideas as to how this or that happened, but for the most part I still have many black holes regarding these events that I cannot answer in my mind. But this much I have learned and accepted; in this life there are, and will be, events and happenings that cannot be explained.

Looking back to some of my past experiences may help shed some light as to how I became prepared for the two major jobs which I did while in Berlin, – overseeing the long lines communication and installing a new radio broadcast station.

1) When I was four years old we lived in Spokane, Washington. On occasion, my mother would let me stay up late. We would sit at the dining room table, and she would adjust the cat's whisker and coil on the crystal set until she got a radio station as loud as she could get it, tuning the little sliding arm on the crystal set. When she got a station, she put the earphones on my head. One night I heard a man in the headphones say, "This is KDKA Pittsburg (Pennsylvania)."

Four years old with my Dad

"Mother, where is Pittsburg?

"George, it is a long, long ways from here."

"Is it as far as Liberty Lake?"

"No George, it is much farther than Liberty Lake."

Our Model T Ford would take a good part of a day to drive 18 miles to Liberty Lake from Spokane and then back home.

She said, "If we get in the car and drive day and night, we might be able to get there in eight days."

"That's an awful long way."

And at that moment, I decided that I wanted to know how I could hear, in my ears in Spokane, a man talking from that far away. My number one ambition became to learn how this worked. This curiosity took me through studies of physics, matter, mass, energy, space and time, science, engineering, electromagnetism generation, transmission, radiation, propagation, and reception. After eighty-five years, I know quite a bit about the physics of how this works, but the most important thing I have learned is that I really know almost nothing about it at all! No joke!!

2) First, I built crystal sets. I thought maybe I could make a better one than the one we had. I started by winding coils to make the cat's whisker to see if I could tune in the station better to get a clearer sound. I made quite a few crystal sets that worked quite well using these coils. Then I build a one tube radio which worked even better than any crystal set, producing a louder and clear sound. My radio consisted of a bread board with a tube socket for holding a vacuum tube and some other parts and wire that I used to solder the parts together. Next I put an audio amplifier on by adding another vacuum tube to the bread board, which produced a louder sound in the headphones. Then I added a third tube, so that I had enough amplification that I could run a loud speaker instead of listening with my headphones.

3) My Dad was a motorcycle policeman, and he was provided with one of the first two-way medium wave radios used by the Spokane Police department. A fellow officer who was in charge of the police radio system loaned me a 1924 book on how to build radio receivers and transmitters. I used it to learn how to build my own. When people learned of my interest in radio, they gave me their old broken radios so I could use the parts.

4) Shortwave was just becoming known as I was growing up. I found a magazine, most likely a Popular Science, which explained how to build a shortwave radio receiver. I built one and started listening to radio stations all over the world. Boy, was this exciting to me!

5) Next I learned how to make audio amplifiers. Most phonographs of the day were mechanical phonographs, and I learned how to make a transducer that would pick up the variations in the record as it spun around, turn it into electrical energy, run it into my audio amplifier, and then play it in my headphones. That sounded a lot better than the mechanical phonograph. Then I built my own phonographs. Next, I progressed to building a recorder. The first one I built I called "the basher," because I would use a pre-grooved soft record with nothing on it. When I recorded someone speaking or playing a musical instrument with my recorder, it would "bash" the sides of the grooves to record the sound.

6) My friend, Dick Collard, and I each built a 2 meter transceiver, and we set up an antenna at each of our homes so we could talk back and forth to each other. Not too long after we start talking, a man joined our conversation and said "Hey you boys, do you have a license to operate

your radios?"

"No," we said. "What's a license?"

He said, "You have to have a license in order to operate that thing you are operating."

Boy, that was a shock to us. We had successfully built our radios, and now we could not use them without getting a license. This man invited us over to his house and explained what we needed to do to get our amateur radio license. We were disappointed. In order to get the license, we had to learn a lot of technical information about Amateur Radio. We had to demonstrate that we could send Morse Code at 10 words a minute. So we practiced and practiced sending code. We got the amateur radio license manual, and we studied and studied. At that time, a local amateur could give the test, so this man gave us the test. We passed and received a class C license, which was the lowest class at the time. We got back on our amateur radios, and now we were in seventh heaven, talking back and forth with each other.

While we studying for test, we learned that there were other amateur radio "bands" where you could talk all over the world. I kept building more and more receivers and transmitters until I had one that was up to 250 watts power on all the bands, and I was talking to people from around the world and having a great time on amateur radio.

7) While in my junior year in high school in 1938, Dick Collard, whose called signal was W7FKL, and I discovered that VHF radio waves reflected off of airplanes.

We each had a receiver that had a meter, something like a field intensity meter, on our amateur radio station. One day while Dick and I were talking, we noticed that the needle on the meters, would start moving, at first just a little bit. Its range of movement would get wider and wider until it was wildly moving all the way from one end of the meter to the other. And then it reversed the process until it just barely moving in the center and then the needle stopped.

We wondered what caused this needle to start moving and then stop. One of us noticed that there was an airplane flying by when this happened. So, we starting checking each time the needle starting moving and indeed found that each time the needle moved an airplane was flying by. We had discovered that radio waves were reflected off of airplanes. Using only this signal strength meter, we could calculate how far away the plane was, how fast it was traveling, and in what direction. We started calculating with what little math we knew at the time and figured out that the plane was about 30 miles away when needle first started to move. We named this system "The Airplane Detector." This was about 10 years before the term "Radar" came to be.

8) I was so excited by this discovery that I wrote it up and sent it to the head of the United States Invention Department (a man named Reynolds) in Washington, D.C. I receive no response from the Invention Department. Obviously a high school student, writing a technical report of this type, with the report being quite crude, it was ignored.

At this time England was being badly bombed by the German Luftwaffe. Their only defense was big aural audio ears, good for much less than 30 miles. Our Airplane Detector would protect them so much better than their current defense system. Therefore, I mailed my report to England.

Soon after that, there was knock on our front door and my dad answered. The man asked, "Are you Mr. Frese?"

"Yes."

"I'm with the FBI, and you are under arrest."

My father was a city policeman for the Spokane Police Department and a very devoted and honest person.

"What are the charges?"

"Sending military information to England. They are at war, and the United States is a neutral country."

"You have the wrong man, but let me call my son down here and see if he knows anything about this."

"Son, do you know anything about sending military information to England?"

"Sure, Dad, I did that."

The FBI man looked down at me and said, "Mr. Frese, you should keep better track of what your son is doing." and he left.

A little later, the Invention Department set up a military test of our Airplane Detector method in what was called the North/South Carolina Airplane Maneuvers. Planes flew from North Carolina into South Carolina, and none of the planes got through without being detected. They sent me a letter telling me that they had done this test. I have long since lost that letter.

9) All of my high school and college studies of physics, science, electricity, chemistry, and others were based on how electromagnetic energy works.

10) I had not noticed until I graduated from college, that of the 400 men who started the engineering program at Washington State University when I was a freshman, there were only seven of us left. Four of these men were handicapped and were not fit for military service. The other two had specific jobs waiting for them. Bob Jepson went to work at the Hanford Research Center in Richland, Washington. Dick Harbor became a professor at WSU. As for the rest of the 400 men, some flunked out, some changed their major, but many of them either enlisted or were drafted in the war.

When I was a freshman in college, a military recruiter came to our campus and talked with Professor F.H. Licky, who was in charge of the engineering program. I had told my professor about my discovery of the Airplane Detector. I suspect that he told the recruiter about this. The recruiter talked with me, and I signed an agreement that as long as I maintained a B average I would be allowed to remain in college. So, I was not drafted when most of my fellow students were.

I actually forgot about having signed this agreement for the rest of my time at Washington State University. I don't know exactly what it said, because the recruiter explained it to me, and I signed it without actually reading it myself.

11) I received my draft notice the day before my graduation from Washington State University.

By the time I entered the Army in June 1944, I was well steeped in some specific areas of science and engineering. I had graduated from Washington State University with a BS degree in Engineering. I believe now that some information about my "Airplane Detection" discovery and my engineering background must have shown up on my early military records.

12) About ten to fifteen years ago, I watched a television special about a top secret project that took place at Massachusetts Institute of Technology in Cambridge, Massachusetts, during World War II. It was a project to research and develop a radar system. I was extremely interested in this show. I realized after watching this show that the military's involvement with this project ended shortly before I graduated from Officers Candidate School (OCS). The big question that this brought into my thought was, "Could there have been a plan for me to work on this project before the military involvement was no longer needed? When I graduated from OCS, was I supposed to be assigned to this radar project as Military officer?"

13) I believe that there are two items on one's military dossier that determine where an Army officer can be assigned.

   a. The officer's rank (Lieutenant, Major, Colonel, General).

   b. Qualifications for specific jobs. I don't know what was in my dossier, but my qualifications for a specific job were probably very high in one specific area.

     I do know that when I took the intelligence test at the Reception Center upon entering the Army, my score was 170, which is the highest score that one could receive.

I have reason to suspect that my airplane detector experience was also in my records.

Could it be that my rank and my specific qualifications were never compatible with any possible military assignment? Did I happen to fall in a crack in the Military law book? Was there something not properly covered in the U.S. Military Organizational Code of Law so that even a General could not provide a solution and give me an assignment?

All of the above questions fall into my "WHY" category. These are questions that probably never will be answered. I have carried this mystery around with me since my discharge: Why could I not be given an assignment by anyone? I realize that this is a WHY question, and that it is not worth worrying about. I should just let it go and find the peace of mind that comes from laying the question to rest.

Through all of this, I have finally decided WHY all things happen. It is because God planned it that way from the beginning. And by believing that, I have even more peace of mind.

In the military, I was set apart for some reason that was unknown to me then, and is still unknown to me today. This is a strong case for Divine Providence and Intervention. My father wrote an autobiography of his life beginning at age 4 and ending at his death at age 90. It is titled, "Nothing Just Happens." Amen. My father and I, near the end of our lives, have reached the same conclusion. His autobiography has been published, and there is a copy in all large city, county, state, and federal police libraries in the United States. Dad's autobiography has been an inspiration for me.

My Dad, Fred Frese, a Spokane police officer

Appendix A
Military Records

I recently learned that I could request my military records. I was hoping that these records would shed some light on this mystery. But unfortunately, my records were destroyed in a fire in 1973. The following image of the letter I received shows this. It also shows that I was discharged as a Second Lieutenant.

National Personnel Records Center

Military Personnel Records, *9700 Page Avenue St. Louis, Missouri 63132-5100*

September 14, 2011

GEORGE FRESE
656 N. MILLER ST.
WENATCHEE, WA 98801

RE: Veteran's Name: FRESE, George M
SN: 01 651 264
Request Number: 1-9755430901

Dear Sir:

The record needed to answer your inquiry is not in our files. If the record were here on July 12, 1973, it would have been in the area that suffered the most damage in the fire on that date and may have been destroyed. The fire destroyed the major portion of records of Army military personnel for the period 1912 through 1959, and records of Air Force personnel with surnames Hubbard through Z for the period 1947 through 1963. Fortunately, there are alternate records sources that often contain information which can be used to reconstruct service record data lost in the fire; however, **complete records cannot be reconstructed**.

We are pleased to enclose NA Form 13038, *Certification of Military Service*. This document verifies military service and may be used for any official purpose. A seal has been affixed to this document to attest to its authenticity. The information used to prepare the enclosed NA Form 13038 was obtained from an alternate record source.

If you have questions or comments regarding this response, you may contact us at 314-801-0800 or by mail at the address shown in the letterhead above. If you contact us, please reference the Request Number listed above. If you are a veteran, or a deceased veteran's next of kin, please consider submitting your future requests online by visiting us at http://vetrecs.archives.gov.

Sincerely,

DAVID L. JOHNSON
Archives Technician (2A)

Enclosure(s)

**We Value Our
Veterans' Privacy**
*Let us know if we have
failed to protect it.*

Certification of
Military Service

****

This certifies that George M. Frese
01 651 264

was a member of the Army of the United States

from March 2, 1945

to October 8, 1946

Service was terminated by Honorable Relief from Active Duty

Last Grade, Rank, or Rating Second Lieutenant

Active Service Dates Same As Above

Date of Birth: 6/5/1921 Place of Birth: N/A
Prior active enlisted service(19143120) from September 25, 1942 to
March 1, 1945 Honorable Discharge to accept Commission

*************** National Personnel Records Center
(Military Personnel Records)
Given at St. Louis, Missouri on September 12, 2011 National Archives and Records Administration

THE ARCHIVIST OF THE UNITED STATES IS THE PHYSICAL CUSTODIAN OF THIS PERSON'S MILITARY RECORD

This Certification of Military Service is issued in the absence of a copy of the actual Report of Separation or its equivalent. This document serves as verification of military service and may be used for any official purpose. Not valid without official seal.

Appendix B
Map Used in Europe

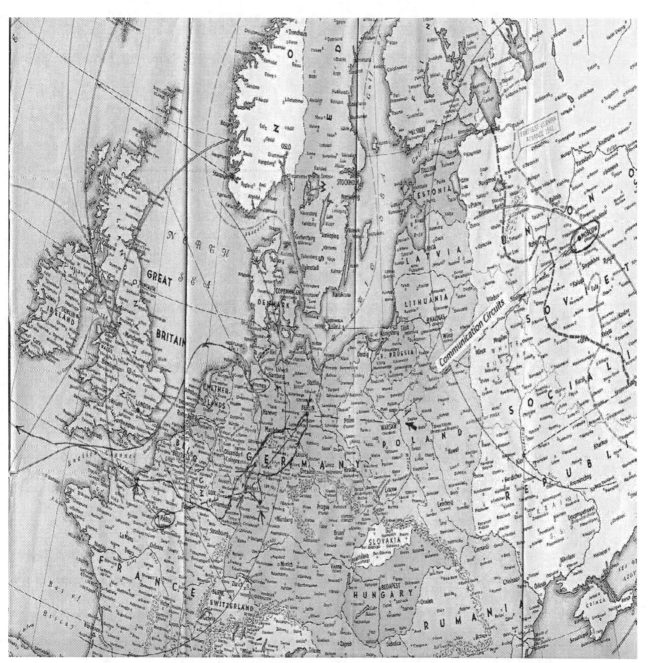

My map I had while in Europe
A little distorted in this view

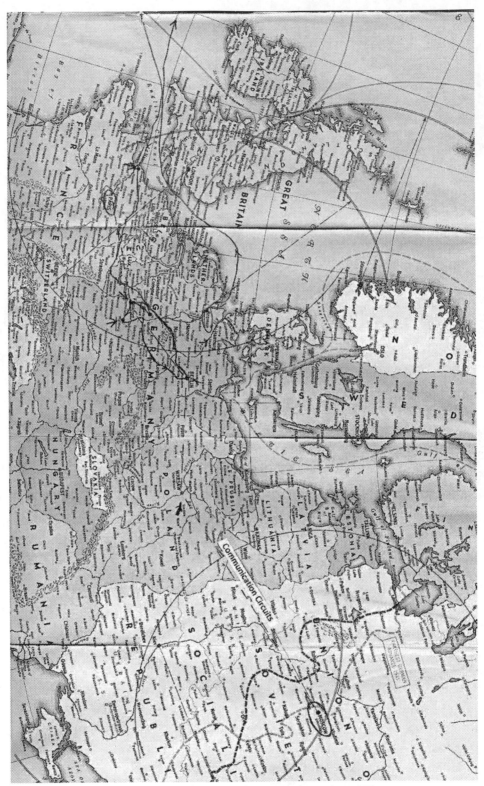

This is more what the maps looks like

Appendix C
More Pictures

Going to church

Brandenburg Gate after the war
This is the gate that divided East and West Berlin

Near the Russian sector

From a streetcar in the Russian sector

Kaiser Wilhelm church

Berlin streetcar

Berlin street

On the streets of Berlin

A market in Berlin

Operators manning the telephone lines in Farnamt building

Local city switchboard in the Farnamt building

Roy Weise, myself, and Bud Spalding

3110 Signal Corp Battalion headquarters

3110 Signal Corp Battalion side gate

Headquarters of Long Lines 3160 Signal Service Battalion

Sign for 3160 Line Lines in Berlin

Chaplin's office

Kitchen sink in my apartment

Sports Palace in Berlin

Armed Forces Network in Frankfort

Streetcar in Frankfort